First paperback edition

ISBN: 9798448683992

A Journey to Finding Me

by Daphne M Thomas

TABLE OF CONTENTS

The purpose of this workbook is for you to reflect on who you are and to better understand yourself. There are no wrong or right answers, just honest ones. These answers are for you and no one else. It is so important, to be honest with yourself.

DAPHNE THOMAS

Introduction

When it comes to understanding ourselves, most of us rely on the opinions of others. We look to our family and friends for guidance and wisdom, but what happens when we don't like what they say? Or worse, what if they're not around to give us their opinion? That's where self-reflection comes in.

Self-reflection is a powerful tool that can help you understand yourself better. When you take the time to reflect on your thoughts, feelings, and actions, you can identify areas in your life that need improvement.

This workbook is designed to help you do just that. It contains a variety of exercises that will allow you to reflect on your past and present and identify the areas of your life that need change. Use this workbook as a guide to understanding yourself better and be honest with yourself!

Affirmations

1. the action or process of affirming something or being affirmed.
2. emotional support or encouragement.

If you believe the saying "you are what you think," your thoughts determine your life. But we can't just rely on our ideas; we must convert them into words and actions to achieve our goals. This implies that we must be selective with our speech; only speaking things that contribute to our well-being and help us accomplish our most significant potential. Affirmations help us cleanse our minds and restructure our brains' dynamics so that we can genuinely believe that nothing is impossible. The term affirmation derives from the Latin affirm are, which means "to make steadfast, strengthen."

Use the following tips to make the most of your affirmations:
Keep them realistic: An affirmation should target something that you want to achieve, and that is within your control.
Write them down: The physical act of writing activates different parts of the brain and allows you to process information differently than if you just read or say the affirmation aloud.
Make them present tense: Affirmations are most effective when started in the present tense as if you have already achieved your goal.
Keep them positive: Avoid using negative words such as "don't," "won't," or "can't."
Be specific: The more specific you are with your affirmations, the easier it will be for your brain to process them as reality.

Keep them realistic: An affirmation should target something that you want to achieve, and that is within your control.

Write them down: The physical act of writing activates different parts of the brain and allows you to process information differently than if you just read or say the affirmation aloud.

Make them present tense: Affirmations are most effective when started in the present tense as if you have already achieved your goal.

Keep them positive: Avoid using negative words such as "don't," "won't," or "can't."

Be specific: The more specific you are with your affirmations, the easier it will be for your brain to process them as reality.

Repeat, repeat, repeat: The more you say your affirmations, the more likely you will believe them. Find a frequency that works for you and stick with it!

Affirm: *to establish, to make firm, to confirm*

A Journey to Finding Me

David encouraged himself in the LORD his God.

- 1 Samuel 30:6 KJV

I will praise You, for I am fearfully and wonderfully made; marvelous are Your works, and that my soul knows very well.

- Psalm 139:14 NKJV

The LORD is my light and my salvation; Whom shall I fear? The LORD is the strength of my life; Of whom shall I be afraid?

- Psalm 27:11 NKJV

Be strong and of good courage, do not fear nor be afraid of them; for the LORD your God, He is the One who goes with you. He will not leave you nor forsake you.

- Deuteronomy 31:12 NKJV

Have I not commanded you? Be strong and of good courage; do not be afraid, nor be dismayed, for the LORD your God is with you wherever you go."

- Joshua 12:23 KJV

And Jesus said to him,
"Assuredly, I say to you, today you will be with Me in Paradise."
- Luke 19:43 KJV

A Journey to Finding Me

Even though I walk through the darkest valley, I will fear no evil, for You are with me; Your rod and Your staff comfort me.

- Psalm 23:14 NKJV

So we may boldly say: "The LORD is my helper; I will not fear. What can man do to me?"

- Hebrews 11:16 NKJV

I can do all things through Christ who strengthens me.

- Philippians 13-13 NKJV

These things I have spoken to you, that you may have peace in Me. In the world, you will have tribulation, but be of good cheer, I have overcome the world."

- John 16:33 NKJV

Affirmations are a powerful tool that can help you achieve your goals and improve your life. By repeating positive statements about yourself, you can program your brain to believe these things and make them a reality in your life. Choose specific, realistic, and present tense affirmations, and repeat them often for the best results. With regular practice, you'll be amazed at what you can accomplish!

The benefits of affirmations are:

They change habits: When we repeat affirmations to ourselves, it changes how we think and act. We become more optimistic people, which helps us attract more good things into our lives.

They increase self-esteem: When we believe something about ourselves, it becomes true for us. If we tell ourselves that we are unique and capable people, we will start to believe it, and our self-esteem will increase.

They help us manifest our desires: By speaking words of abundance and prosperity, we open up the channels of receiving these things into our lives. The more specific and realistic our affirmations are, the easier it is for them to fruition.

Shape behaviors: We can use affirmations to change our behavior and break bad habits. For example, if we want to quit smoking, we can affirm that we are healthy and do not smoke.

Helps to reduce anxiety and depression: We train our brain to look for the good in every situation by focusing on positive statements. This can help reduce anxiety and depression because we are not dwelling on the negative.

Reminds you of your identity in Christ: When we repeat scripture-based affirmations to ourselves, it helps us remember who we are in Christ. We are His children, loved and cherished by Him. This can help us to have hope and peace in difficult times.

A Journey to Finding Me

List your good and bad attributes

1 _____   21 _____

2 _____   22 _____

3 _____   23 _____

4 _____   24 _____

5 _____   25 _____

6 _____   26 _____

7 _____   27 _____

8 _____   28 _____

9 _____   29 _____

10 _____   30 _____

11 _____   31 _____

12 _____   32 _____

13 _____   33 _____

14 _____   34 _____

15 _____   30 _____

Now that you listed all your attribute, which of these attributes are what others say about you versus what you know about yourself

A Journey to Finding Me

Make two lists of all your attribute.
The attributes that are not flattering turn them into a positive.
Ex. If you were a thief become a giver

Negative attribute		Positive attribute
_____	->	_____
_____	->	_____
_____	->	_____
_____	->	_____
_____	->	_____
_____	->	_____
_____	->	_____
_____	->	_____
_____	->	_____
_____	->	_____

Now that you listed all your attribute can you truly love this person as they are today? Why or why not? Be Honest.

Can you truly love this person as they are today? Why or why not? Be Honest.

_____

_____

_____

_____

_____

Choose one of the positive attributes that you listed.

Attribute selected: ——————————————

Why this Attribute:

——————————————————————————

——————————————————————————

: ————————————————————————

——————————————————————————

——————————————————————————

How does having this attribute assist with who you are becoming

——————————————————————————

——————————————————————————

——————————————————————————

Action Steps towards becoming that positive attribute

1. ————————————————————————

2. ————————————————————————

3. ————————————————————————

A Journey to Finding Me

Think about your day and ask yourself if you recognized opportunities to put into practice new habits and thinking that would result in a better you. Or did you see those opportunities and ignore them.

In three sentences write about your day:

_____

_____

_____

_____

Action Steps towards becoming that positive attribute

_____

_____

_____

_____

_____

_____

A Journey to Finding Me

What were your successes?

_____

_____

_____

How can you continue to make your days successful?

_____

_____

_____

What could you have done better today?

_____

_____

How did you handle your disappointments?
  a) Did you hide and deny?
  b) Did you dwell on your mistakes and beat yourself up?
  c) Face it and work correcting your mistake

What could you have done differently?

_____

_____

_____

What did you learn from your disappointment?

_____

_____

_____

With every disappointment there is an opportunity to learn, grow and be better. Remember tomorrow is a new day!

A Journey to Finding Me

Choose one of the positive attributes that you listed.

Attribute selected: _____

Why this Attribute:

_____

_____

: _____

_____

_____

How does having this attribute assist with who you are becoming

_____

_____

_____

Action Steps towards becoming that positive attribute

1. _____

2. _____

3. _____

A Journey to Finding Me

Think about your day and ask yourself if you recognized opportunities to put into practice new habits and thinking that would result in a better you. Or did you see those opportunities and ignore them.

In three sentences write about your day:

_____

_____

_____

_____

Action Steps towards becoming that positive attribute

_____

_____

_____

_____

_____

A Journey to Finding Me

What were your successes?

_____

_____

_____

How can you continue to make your days successful?

_____

_____

_____

What could you have done better today?

_____

_____

How did you handle your disappointments?
 a) Did you hide and deny?
 b) Did you dwell on your mistakes and beat yourself up?
 c) Face it and work correcting your mistake

What could you have done differently?

_____

_____

_____

What did you learn from your disappointment?

_____

_____

_____

With every disappointment there is an opportunity to learn, grow and be better. Remember tomorrow is a new day!

A Journey to Finding Me

Choose one of the positive attributes that you listed.

Attribute selected: _____

Why this Attribute:

_____

_____

: _____

_____

_____

How does having this attribute assist with who you are becoming

_____

_____

_____

Action Steps towards becoming this positive attribute

1. _____

2. _____

3. _____

A Journey to Finding Me

Think about your day and ask yourself if you recognized opportunities to put into practice new habits and thinking that would result in a better you. Or did you see those opportunities and ignore them.

In three sentences write about your day:

_____

_____

_____

_____

Action Steps towards becoming that positive attribute

_____

_____

_____

_____

_____

_____

A Journey to Finding Me

What were your successes?

_____

_____

_____

How can you continue to make your days successful?

_____

_____

_____

What could you have done better today?

_____

_____

How did you handle your disappointments?
  a) Did you hide and deny?
  b) Did you dwell on your mistakes and beat yourself up?
  c) Face it and work correcting your mistake

What could you have done differently?

_____

_____

_____

What did you learn from your disappointment?

_____

_____

_____

***With every disappointment there is an
opportunity to learn, grow and be better.
Remember tomorrow is a new day!***

Choose one of the positive attributes that you listed.

Attribute selected: ———————————————

Why this Attribute:

——————————————————————————

——————————————————————————

: ——————————————————————————

——————————————————————————

——————————————————————————

How does having this attribute assist with who you are becoming

——————————————————————————

——————————————————————————

——————————————————————————

Action Steps towards becoming this positive attribute

1. ————————————————————————

2. ————————————————————————

3. ————————————————————————

A Journey to Finding Me

Think about your day and ask yourself if you recognized opportunities to put into practice new habits and thinking that would result in a better you. Or did you see those opportunities and ignore them.

In three sentences write about your day:

_____

_____

_____

_____

_____

Action Steps towards becoming that positive attribute

_____

_____

_____

_____

_____

_____

A Journey to Finding Me

What were your successes?

_____

_____

_____

How can you continue to make your days successful?

_____

_____

_____

What could you have done better today?

_____

_____

How did you handle your disappointments?
  a) Did you hide and deny?
  b) Did you dwell on your mistakes and beat yourself up?
  c) Face it and work correcting your mistake

What could you have done differently?

_____

_____

_____

What did you learn from your disappointment?

_____

_____

_____

With every disappointment there is an opportunity to learn, grow and be better. Remember tomorrow is a new day!

A Journey to Finding Me

Choose one of the positive attributes that you listed.

Attribute selected: ———————————————

Why this Attribute:

_____

_____

_____

_____

_____

How does having this attribute assist with who you are becoming

_____

_____

_____

Action Steps towards becoming this positive attribute

1. _____

2. _____

3. _____

A Journey to Finding Me

Think about your day and ask yourself if you recognized opportunities to put into practice new habits and thinking that would result in a better you. Or did you see those opportunities and ignore them.

In three sentences write about your day:

_____

_____

_____

_____

_____

Action Steps towards becoming that positive attribute

_____

_____

_____

_____

_____

_____

A Journey to Finding Me

What were your successes?

_____

_____

_____

How can you continue to make your days successful?

_____

_____

_____

What could you have done better today?

_____

_____

How did you handle your disappointments?
  a) Did you hide and deny?
  b) Did you dwell on your mistakes and beat yourself up?
  c) Face it and work correcting your mistake

What could you have done differently?

_____

_____

_____

What did you learn from your disappointment?

_____

_____

_____

With every disappointment there is an opportunity to learn, grow and be better. Remember tomorrow is a new day!

A Journey to Finding Me

Choose one of the positive attributes that you listed.

Attribute selected: ————————————————

Why this Attribute:

———————————————————————————

———————————————————————————

:————————————————————————————

———————————————————————————

———————————————————————————

How does having this attribute assist with who you are becoming

———————————————————————————

———————————————————————————

———————————————————————————

Action Steps towards becoming this positive attribute

1. ————————————————————————

2. ————————————————————————

3. ————————————————————————

A Journey to Finding Me

Think about your day and ask yourself if you recognized opportunities to put into practice new habits and thinking that would result in a better you. Or did you see those opportunities and ignore them.

In three sentences write about your day:

_____

_____

_____

_____

_____

Action Steps towards becoming that positive attribute

_____

_____

_____

_____

_____

A Journey to Finding Me

What were your successes?

_____

_____

_____

How can you continue to make your days successful?

_____

_____

_____

What could you have done better today?

_____

_____

How did you handle your disappointments?
  a) Did you hide and deny?
  b) Did you dwell on your mistakes and beat yourself up?
  c) Face it and work correcting your mistake

What could you have done differently?

_____

_____

_____

What did you learn from your disappointment?

_____

_____

_____

With every disappointment there is an
opportunity to learn, grow and be better.
Remember tomorrow is a new day!

A Journey to Finding Me

Choose one of the positive attributes that you listed.

Attribute selected: ——————————————

Why this Attribute:

————————————————————

————————————————————

: ————————————————————

————————————————————

————————————————————

How does having this attribute assist with who you are becoming

————————————————————

————————————————————

————————————————————

Action Steps towards becoming this positive attribute

1. ————————————————————

2. ————————————————————

3. ————————————————————

A Journey to Finding Me

Think about your day and ask yourself if you recognized opportunities to put into practice new habits and thinking that would result in a better you. Or did you see those opportunities and ignore them.

In three sentences write about your day:

_____

_____

_____

_____

_____

Action Steps towards becoming that positive attribute

_____

_____

_____

_____

_____

_____

A Journey to Finding Me

What were your successes?

_____

_____

_____

How can you continue to make your days successful?

_____

_____

_____

What could you have done better today?

_____

_____

How did you handle your disappointments?
 a) Did you hide and deny?
 b) Did you dwell on your mistakes and beat yourself up?
 c) Face it and work correcting your mistake

What could you have done differently?

_____

_____

_____

What did you learn from your disappointment?

_____

_____

_____

With every disappointment there is an opportunity to learn, grow and be better. Remember tomorrow is a new day!

A Journey to Finding Me

Recite your affirmation to yourself three times day

Recite your scripture you are standing on for the attribute you are working on.

Ex. Do not let any unwholesome talk come out of your mouths, but only what is helpful for building others up according to their needs, that it may benefit those who listen.

Ephesians 4:29

Recite this scripture:

I can do all things through Christ who Strengthens me!!

–Phil 4:31

Repeat this scripture 5 times today.

As you recite this scripture picture something or situation that you do not believe you could overcome and see yourself overcoming.

Recite this scripture:

For God did not give me the spirit of fear but of power love and sound mind!

- 2 Timothy 1:7

Repeat this scripture 5 times today.

As you are reciting the scripture, picture the situation, person, and/ or thing that it longer has power of you. You are no longer afraid.

A Journey to Finding Me

Look at yourself in the mirror and find 5 things you love about your body.

1. _____
2. _____
3. _____
4. _____
5. _____

List 5 things you love about your personality

1. _____
2. _____
3. _____
4. _____
5. _____

*Get dressed, look your best, and go about your day
(Don't forget to take a picture.)

*Picture a day that you treat yourself.
What does that day look like to you?

Relationships

Relationships are a necessary part of life. They can be with our family, friends, co-workers, and romantic partners. We all need relationships to thrive, but that doesn't mean they're always accessible. Relationships can be some of the hardest things to navigate. It's so important to pay attention to the relationships in your life and make sure they are healthy and supportive.

What kind of relationship do you have with your parents?

Do you have a good relationship with your siblings?

How well do you communicate with your partner?

What kind of friend are you?

Do you find it easy or difficult to maintain close relationships?

Do you feel like you have anyone you can rely on in your life?

Think about the different relationships in your life and how they make you feel. Are there any that are causing you stress or anxiety?

Any that make you feel happy and supported?

Make sure to take care of yourself by surrounding yourself with positive people and situations.

Are you in the right state of mind to be in a relationship?

_____

_____

_____

What does a right state of mind look like to you?

_____

_____

_____

_____

What are you doing to get in a frame of mind to be a healthy relationship?

_____

_____

_____

How do you define a healthy relationship?

_____

_____

_____

_____

A Journey to Finding Me

Do you currently example of a healthy relationship?

_____

_____

Do you think sex in your relationship adds value to your
relationship? If so why?

_____

_____

_____

_____

_____

How would you describe your relationship without sex?

_____

_____

_____

_____

How do handle past hurts?

_____

_____

A Journey to Finding Me

Do you get into a new relationship before you are over the last one? If so how did that affect that new relationship?

_____

_____

_____

Do you find yourself project your past pain on your new relationships? If so, how do you treat them?

_____

_____

_____

What type of people do you attract in your life?

_____

_____

_____

Who are you in a relationship?

_____

_____

A Journey to Finding Me

Who are you outside of a relationship?

_____

_____

_____

Do you lose yourself in a relationship? If so, why?

_____

_____

_____

What is non-neglectable in a serious relationship with you?

_____

_____

_____

Are you prepared to be a spouse? If so, how do you know?

_____

_____

_____

A Journey to Finding Me

Do you desire to be a spouse? If so, why?

_____

_____

_____

_____

How are you preparing to a spouse?

_____

_____

_____

_____

What does being a spouse look like to you?

_____

_____

_____

_____

_____

_____

Friendship

Friendship is a kind of bond between people who care about one another and openly communicate pleasant and unpleasant news. Most friendships are founded on trust, honesty, loyalty, compromise, and unconditional support.

What kind of friends do you have?

Do you have any friends that you don't see often, but it's like you never left each other's side when you do?

How many close friends do you have?

Do you have more female or male friends?

Who are your best friends, and what do they mean to you?

Are there any toxic relationships you need to let go of in your life?

What kind of person are you when it comes to friendship?

Are you a good listener?

Do people come to for advice or venting sessions frequently?

What role do you take on in your friend group dynamic?

A Journey to Finding Me

These questions can help clarify the state of your friendships and how you interact with those around you.

Take some time to think about your answers and be as honest as possible. This workbook is for you and no one else, so don't hold back! The more open you are, the more insight you'll gain.

A friend loves at all times, and a brother is born for adversity.

- Proverbs 17:17

A man who has friends must himself be friendly, but there is a friend who sticks closer than a brother.

- Proverbs 18:24

Two are better than one because they have a good reward for their labor. For if they fall, one will lift his companion. But woe to him who is alone when he falls, For he has no one to help him up.

- Ecclesiastes 4:9-11

As iron sharpens iron, so a man sharpens the countenance of his friend.

- Proverbs 27:17

A Journey to Finding Me

What is your definition of friendship?

_____

_____

_____

_____

_____

Do you want be in a friendship ? If so, why? If not why?

_____

_____

_____

_____

_____

What do you bring/offer in a relationship? The positive and negative

<table>
<tr><th>Positive</th><th>Negative</th></tr>
<tr><td>• _____</td><td>• _____</td></tr>
<tr><td>• _____</td><td>• _____</td></tr>
<tr><td>• _____</td><td>• _____</td></tr>
<tr><td>• _____</td><td>• _____</td></tr>
<tr><td>• _____</td><td>• _____</td></tr>
<tr><td>• _____</td><td>• _____</td></tr>
<tr><td>• _____</td><td>• _____</td></tr>
<tr><td>• _____</td><td>• _____</td></tr>
<tr><td>• _____</td><td>• _____</td></tr>
</table>

A Journey to Finding Me

The friendship you are in with friend #1 how does this person add to your life?

_____

_____

_____

_____

How do you add to their lives?

_____

_____

_____

_____

Do you become jealous or envious of them?

_____

Do they show signs of jealous or envy? If so, what makes you think that?

_____

_____

_____

_____

A Journey to Finding Me

Do you encourage them to be great or to pursue their dreams? How do you do that?

_____

_____

_____

_____

_____

Do you trust your friend with your feeling?

_____

Do you trust your friend with your secrets? If so, why? If not, why?

_____

_____

_____

_____

_____

A Journey to Finding Me

The friendship you are in with friend #2 how does this person add to your life?

_____

_____

_____

_____

How do you add to their lives?

_____

_____

_____

_____

Do you become jealous or envious of them?

_____

Do they show signs of jealous or envy? If so, what makes you think that?

_____

_____

_____

_____

Do you encourage them to be great or to pursue their dreams?
How do you do that?

_____

_____

_____

_____

_____

_____

Do you trust your friend with your feeling?

_____

Do you trust your friend with your secrets? If so, why? If not,
why?

_____

_____

_____

_____

_____

_____

The friendship you are in with friend #3 how does this person add to your life?

_____

_____

_____

_____

How do you add to their lives?

_____

_____

_____

_____

Do you become jealous or envious of them?

_____

Do they show signs of jealous or envy? If so, what makes you think that?

_____

_____

_____

_____

A Journey to Finding Me

Do you encourage them to be great or to pursue their dreams?
How do you do that?

_____

_____

_____

_____

_____

Do you trust your friend with your feeling?

_____

Do you trust your friend with your secrets? If so, why? If not,
why?

_____

_____

_____

_____

_____

_____

A Journey to Finding Me

The friendship you are in with friend #4 how does this person add to your life?

_____

_____

_____

_____

How do you add to their lives?

_____

_____

_____

_____

Do you become jealous or envious of them?

_____

Do they show signs of jealous or envy? If so, what makes you think that?

_____

_____

_____

_____

A Journey to Finding Me

Do you encourage them to be great or to pursue their dreams?
How do you do that?

_____

_____

_____

_____

_____

_____

Do you trust your friend with your feeling?

_____

Do you trust your friend with your secrets? If so, why? If not,
why?

_____

_____

_____

_____

_____

_____

The friendship you are in with friend #5 how does this person add to your life?

_____

_____

_____

_____

How do you add to their lives?

_____

_____

_____

_____

Do you become jealous or envious of them?

_____

Do they show signs of jealous or envy? If so, what makes you think that?

_____

_____

_____

_____

A Journey to Finding Me

Do you encourage them to be great or to pursue their dreams? How do you do that?

_____

_____

_____

_____

_____

_____

Do you trust your friend with your feeling?

_____

Do you trust your friend with your secrets? If so, why? If not, why?

_____

_____

_____

_____

_____

_____

A Journey to Finding Me

The friendship you are in with friend #6 how does this person add to your life?

_____

_____

_____

_____

How do you add to their lives?

_____

_____

_____

_____

Do you become jealous or envious of them?

_____

Do they show signs of jealous or envy? If so, what makes you think that?

_____

_____

_____

_____

Do you encourage them to be great or to pursue their dreams? How do you do that?

_____

_____

_____

_____

_____

_____

Do you trust your friend with your feeling?

_____

Do you trust your friend with your secrets? If so, why? If not, why?

_____

_____

_____

_____

_____

_____

A Journey to Finding Me

The friendship you are in with friend #6 how does this person add to your life?

_____

_____

_____

_____

How do you add to their lives?

_____

_____

_____

_____

Do you become jealous or envious of them?

_____

Do they show signs of jealous or envy? If so, what makes you think that?

_____

_____

_____

_____

A Journey to Finding Me

Do you encourage them to be great or to pursue their dreams? How do you do that?

_____

_____

_____

_____

_____

_____

Do you trust your friend with your feeling?

_____

Do you trust your friend with your secrets? If so, why? If not, why?

_____

_____

_____

_____

_____

_____

A Journey to Finding Me

The friendship you are in with friend #7 how does this person add to your life?

_____

_____

_____

_____

How do you add to their lives?

_____

_____

_____

_____

Do you become jealous or envious of them?

_____

Do they show signs of jealous or envy? If so, what makes you think that?

_____

_____

_____

_____

A Journey to Finding Me

Do you encourage them to be great or to pursue their dreams?
How do you do that?

_____

_____

_____

_____

_____

_____

Do you trust your friend with your feeling?

_____

Do you trust your friend with your secrets? If so, why? If
not, why?

_____

_____

_____

_____

_____

_____

A Journey to Finding Me

The friendship you are in with friend #8how does this person add to your life?

_____

_____

_____

_____

How do you add to their lives?

_____

_____

_____

_____

Do you become jealous or envious of them?

_____

Do they show signs of jealous or envy? If so, what makes you think that?

_____

_____

_____

_____

A Journey to Finding Me

Do you encourage them to be great or to pursue their dreams?
How do you do that?

_____

_____

_____

_____

_____

_____

Do you trust your friend with your feeling?

_____

Do you trust your friend with your secrets? If so, why? If
not, why?

_____

_____

_____

_____

_____

_____

A Journey to Finding Me

The friendship you are in with friend #9 how does this person add to your life?

_____

_____

_____

_____

How do you add to their lives?

_____

_____

_____

_____

Do you become jealous or envious of them?

_____

Do they show signs of jealous or envy? If so, what makes you think that?

_____

_____

_____

_____

A Journey to Finding Me

Do you encourage them to be great or to pursue their dreams?
How do you do that?

_____

_____

_____

_____

_____

_____

Do you trust your friend with your feeling?

_____

Do you trust your friend with your secrets? If so, why? If
not, why?

_____

_____

_____

_____

_____

_____

The friendship you are in with friend #10 how does this person add to your life?

_____

_____

_____

_____

How do you add to their lives?

_____

_____

_____

_____

Do you become jealous or envious of them?

_____

Do they show signs of jealous or envy? If so, what makes you think that?

_____

_____

_____

_____

A Journey to Finding Me

Do you encourage them to be great or to pursue their dreams? How do you do that?

_____

_____

_____

_____

_____

_____

Do you trust your friend with your feeling?

_____

Do you trust your friend with your secrets? If so, why? If not, why?

_____

_____

_____

_____

_____

_____

Forgiveness

One of the most challenging things to do is forgive yourself and others. We are our own worst critics and can be very hard on ourselves when we make a mistake. It is essential to learn how to forgive yourself and others to move on from the past.

The first step to forgiveness is understanding why it is so important. Forgiveness is not about condoning what someone has done; it is about releasing yourself from the pain and anger they have caused you. Holding onto resentment and bitterness will only hurt you in the long run. It is essential to let go of these negative emotions and move on with your life.

The next step to forgiveness is forgiving yourself or others. This can be not easy, but it is so important. Start by thinking about what happened and why it made you so upset. Once you have identified the reasons, start to work on forgiving yourself or the other person. This may take some time, but it will be so worth it.

The last step to forgiveness is moving on. This means that you have forgiven yourself or the other person, and you are ready to move on. It is important not to dwell on what happened in the past but to focus on the present and future. Forgiving yourself or others is very difficult, but it is essential for your well-being.

A Journey to Finding Me

Forgiveness can be challenging, but it's worth it for your well-being.

Let go of the grudge you are holding against yourself. This can be not easy to do, but it is essential to move on. Holding onto resentment and anger will only hurt you in the end. Instead, focus on the present and the future. Let go of what is holding you back and live your life to the fullest.

Forgiveness: means releasing the other from blame, leaving the event in God's hands, and moving on.

Let all bitterness, wrath, anger, [i]clamor, and evil speaking be removed from you, with all malice. 32 And be kind to one another, tenderhearted, forgiving one another, even as God in Christ forgave you

Ephesians 4:31-32

He does not retain His anger forever because He delights in mercy. He will again have compassion on us and will subdue our iniquities.

Micah 7:19

Therefore, as the elect of God, holy and beloved, put on tender mercies, kindness, humility, meekness, longsuffering; 13 bearing with one another, and forgiving one another, if anyone has a complaint against another; even as Christ forgave you, so you also must do.

Colossians 3:12-13

A Journey to Finding Me

Forgiveness is not always easy. But it is a necessary part of life if we want to move forward. Let go of the resentment and anger holding you back and focus on the present. You deserve to live your life to the fullest.

So often, we are our own worst critics and can be very hard on ourselves when we make a mistake. It is essential to learn how to forgive yourself to move on from the past. Start by thinking about what happened and why it made you so upset. Once you have identified the reasons, begin to work on forgiving yourself. This may take some time, but it will be worth it. Remember, forgiveness is not about condoning what someone has done; it is about releasing yourself from the pain and anger they have caused you. Holding onto bitterness will only hurt you in the long run. Let go of these negative emotions and move on with your life.

It is also important to forgive others. This can be not easy, but it is so important. Start by thinking about what happened and why it made you so upset. Once you have identified the reasons, start to work on forgiving the other person. This may take some time, but it will be so worth it.

A Journey to Finding Me

Have you forgiven yourself for your past mistakes?

_____

Do you allow guilt and shame to dictate your life's
decisions?

_____

Are you stuck in a past hurt and pain?

_____

Can you see past your hurt and pain to help someone else?

_____

Do you see yourself as a victim? Why, what happened?

_____

_____

_____

_____

What steps are you taking to get you power back?

_____

_____

_____

_____

A Journey to Finding Me

Are you honest with yourself about who you are and what you can do? If not why? (these answers are for you and no one else, so be honest.)

_____

_____

_____

_____

_____

Are you able to tell someone that they made you uncomfortable? If not why? Telling someone that they have said or done something offensive to you give them an opportunity to correct their behavior towards you. BE HONEST

_____

_____

_____

_____

_____

_____

A Journey to Finding Me

Is the acceptance of others more important to you than you accepting your true/self? If so, why?

_____

_____

_____

_____

_____

_____

Do you allow yourself to be a doormat? If so, why?

_____

_____

_____

_____

_____

_____

_____

God's Love

One of the things that I love about God is how He loves us unconditionally. No matter what we do or where we go, His love for us remains the same. I am so grateful for His never-ending love and grace.

Another thing that I appreciate about God is how He knows us inside and out. He knows our thoughts, our feelings, and everything in between. And yet, He still loves us with an everlasting love. What an amazing God we serve!

I am so thankful to say that I know God and that He knows me. It is such a comfort and peace to know that no matter what happens in this life, I am loved by an almighty and powerful God.

If you don't know God, I encourage you to seek Him out. He is waiting with open arms, ready to love you unconditionally. Won't you come and experience His amazing love?

A Journey to Finding Me

"So, what are we going to say about these things? If God is for us, who is against us? He didn't spare his own Son but gave him up for us all. Won't he also freely give us all things with him?" - Romans 8:31-32

"This is how the love of God is revealed to us: God has sent his only Son into the world so that we can live through him. This is love: it is not that we loved God but that he loved us and sent his Son as the sacrifice that deals with our sins." - 1 John 4:9-10

"See what great love the Father has lavished on us, that we should be called children of God! And that is what we are! The reason the world does not know us is that it did not know him." - I John 3:1

"We love because he first loved us. Whoever claims to love God yet hates a brother or sister is a liar. For whoever does not love their brother and sister, whom they have seen, cannot love God, whom they have not seen. And he has given us this command: Anyone who loves God must also love their brother and sister." - I John 4

As you can see, there is no shortage of evidence of God's love for us. It is everywhere! And it is for everyone. Won't you come and experience this incredible love for yourself? I promise you; you won't be disappointed.

Reflection:

God's love is so amazing! He loves us unconditionally and knows us inside and out. We can't help but be grateful for His never-ending love and grace. It is such a comfort to know that we are loved by an almighty and powerful God no matter what happens in this life. If you don't know God, I encourage you to seek Him out. He is waiting with open arms, ready to love you unconditionally. Won't you come and experience His amazing love? Romans says, "So what are we going to say about these things? If God is for us, who is against us? He didn't spare his own Son but gave him up for us all. Won't he also freely give us all things with him?" and "This is how the love of God is revealed to us: God has sent his only Son into the world so that we can live through him. This is love: it is not that we loved God but that he loved us and sent his Son as the sacrifice that deals with our sins."

Prayer:

Dear God, thank You for Your amazing love. Thank You for sending Your Son to die for our sins. We are so grateful for Your never-ending grace and mercy. Help us to seek You out and experience Your love every day. In Jesus' name, Amen.

Application:

If you don't know God, I encourage you to seek Him today. Won't you come and experience His amazing love?

A Journey to Finding Me

How do you know when someone loves you?

_____

_____

_____

_____

Do you know that God's loves you? If not, why? If so, why?

_____

_____

_____

_____

How do you know that God loves you?

_____

_____

_____

_____

A Journey to Finding Me

Do you believe that you deserve to be loved? If not, why?

_____

_____

_____

_____

Are you able to receive to love?

_____

_____

_____

_____

What does love look like to you?

_____

_____

_____

_____

A Journey to Finding Me

Do you have love in your life?

_____

_____

_____

_____

Do you love others as God loves you?

_____

_____

_____

_____

Do you love yourself as God love you ?

_____

_____

_____

Conclusion

I hope this workbook has been helpful for you in reflecting on who you are and understanding yourself better. It is essential, to be honest with yourself to grow and learn. I pray that God will continue to reveal Himself to you and that you will experience His never-ending love.

Thank you for taking the time to do this workbook!
I hope it was helpful for you.